Beru's

SAP FI/CO Interview Questions, Answers, and Explanations

Stuart Lee

Please visit our website at www.sapcookbook.com

© 2006 Equity Press all rights reserved.

ISBN 1-933804-10-6

Trademark notices

SAP, SAP EBP, SAP SRM, Netweaver, and SAP New Dimension are registered trademarks of SAP AG. This publisher gratefully acknowledges SAP permission to use its trademark in this publication. SAP AG is not the publisher of this book and is not responsible for it under any aspect of the law.

TABLE OF CONTENTS

SAP FI/CO Interview Questions

Part I: Accounts Payable (AP)

Question 1: Additional Log

What is the additional log in the AP payment program and how can it be used for troubleshooting ?

A: The additional log is an important setting when performing a payment run. The amount of information stored in the log can be selected (see below).

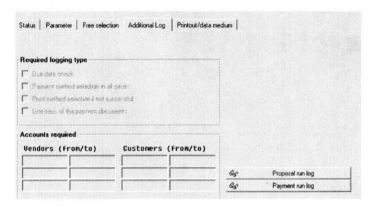

If there are any errors with the payments run, due to either missing or incorrect master data settings, negative balances due to credit memo's etc, the system will report these in the additional log.

Support position interviews often ask this question as a way of determining if you know how to troubleshoot day-to-day Accounts Payable operations.

Question 2: Master Data

How can you link customer and vendor master records and what is the purpose of doing so ?

A: On the customer master there is a field "vendor" and likewise on the vendor master there is a field "customer". By entering these master data numbers, a link can be created between the AP/AR subledgers for use in the payment program, dunning routine and the clearing of open items.

For example in the payment program, if a specific business partner is your vendor but also your customer, linking their master records together will allow the open AR invoices to be offset against the outstanding AP invoices.

Question 3: Payment Terms

What are terms of payments and where are they stored ?

A: Payment terms are created in configuration and determine the payment due date for customer/vendor invoices.

They are stored on the customer/vendor master record and are pulled through onto the customer/vendor invoice postings. The due date derived via the payment can be changed on each individual invoice if required

Question 4: Baseline Date

What is meant by a "baseline date" in SAP AR and AP ?

A: The baseline date is the date from which the payment terms (specified in IMG transaction OBB) apply

Usually this is the document date on the invoice but can also be the date of entry or posting date from the ledger

Question 5: One Time Vendor

What are one-time vendors ?

A: In certain industries (especially where there are a high volume of cash transactions), it is not practical to create new master records for every vendor trading partner.

One-time vendors allow for a dummy vendor code to be used on invoice entry and the information which is normally stored in the vendor master (payment terms, address etc) , is keyed on the invoice itself.

Question 6: AP Vendor Group

What factors should be considered when configuring an Accounts Payable Vendor Group ?

A: The following are determined by the creation of a new AP vendor group (transaction OBD3)

- Whether the vendors in this group are one-time vendors – i.e. no master record is created but the address and payments details are entered against each invoice to this vendor

- Field status group – which fields on the vendor master are suppressed, optional or mandatory when creating vendors belonging to this group

Additionally the vendor number ranges defined in transaction XKN1 need to be assigned to your vendor account groups in transaction OBAS. The decision needs to be made whether to assign an external number range (where the user chooses the master record number) or an internal number range (system assigned)

Question 7: Payment Run

Name the standard stages of the SAP Payment Run.

A: The following steps are usually performed during the payment run

- Entering of parameters (company codes, payment methods, vendor accounts etc)
- Proposal Scheduling – the system proposes list of invoices to be paid
- Payment booking – the booking of the actual payments into the ledger
- Printing of payment forms (cheques etc)

Variations on the above may be found in different SAP customers, but the interviewer will be looking for the basis steps above.

Question 8: Payment Methods

What is the purpose of payment methods and where are they stored?

A: Generally payment methods are one digit alphanumeric identifiers that indicate the type of payments made to vendors or received from customers.

There are many standard delivered SAP entries for each country.

For example for the UK, the following are pre-delivered:-

Country	GB	Great Britain

Payment methods in the country

Pmnt meth.	Name (in language of country)
B	Direct Debit/Standing Order
C	Cheque
D	Direct Deposit (DFS UK)
M	Manual Post /print
S	SWIFT - Transfer
T	Bank transfer
W	Wired payment posting

The payment methods are stored in the vendor/customer master record as well on vendor/customer line items. (The default from master record can be changed during manual postings)

Question 9: Electronic Banking

Explain briefly how you can import electronic bank statements into SAP.

A: A text file is received from the bank which is then uploaded into the SAP system. The file contains details of the company's bank movements e.g. cheques, bank interest, bank charges, cash receipts etc. Depending on the system configuration SAP will attempt to book these transactions automatically to the correct accounts to avoid the need for manual entries by SAP users.

Any postings which the system cannot derive automatically can be booked through "post-processing"

Part II: Accounts Receivable (AR)

Question 10 : Residual Payments

In Accounts Receivable, what's the difference between the 'residual payment' and 'part payment' methods of allocating cash ?

A: These are the two methods for allocating partial payments from customers.

As an example, lets say invoice A123 exists for 100$ and a customer pays 60$.

With partial payment, the 60$ simply offsets the invoice leaving a remaining balance of 40$

With residual payment, invoice A123 is cleared for the full value 100$ and a new invoice line item is booked for the remaining balance of 40$.

Question 11 : Correspondence Types

What are correspondence types in AR/AP ?

A: Correspondence types are different outputs which can be printed and sent to your business partners based around either customer vendor or GL information.

Popular correspondence types include customer statements, payment notices and line items lists. Within the most common AP/AR functions (such as 'Display vendor line items' below there is the option to generate correspondence requests. At the end of the working day these can be printed together as a batch and sent out.

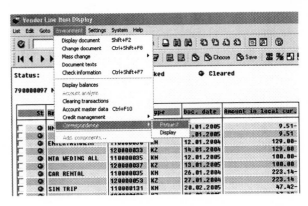

Question 12: Dunning

What is "dunning" in SAP ?

A: Dunning is the process by which payment chasing letters are issued to customers. SAP can determine which customers should receive the letters and for which overdue items.

Different letters can be printed in SAP depending on how far overdue the payment is; from a simple reminder to a legal letter.

The dunning level on the customer master indicates which letter has been issued to the customer.

Question 13 : Reason Codes

What are "reason codes" used for in the Accounts Receivable module and what are the factors to be considered in their configuration?

A: Reason codes are tags which can be assigned to explain under/overpayments during the allocation of incoming customer payments. They should not be confused with 'void reason codes' used when outgoing checks are generated.

During configuration the following are determined

- Whether the items booked with these reason codes are to be flagged as disputed items for the purposes of credit management (disputed items do not increase a customer credit exposure)
- The type of correspondence (if any) to be generated for this reason code as a result of the under/over payment
- Whether a separate line item should be created to charge off the payment differences to a separate G/L account.

_____

Part III: Document Postings

Question 14: Rate factors

What are exchange rate "factors" ?

A: Exchange Rate factors are the relationships between one currency and another to which an exchange rate is applied.

For example you may define the Indonesia Rupiah to US$ factor as 10000 : 1

Combined with an exchange rate of 0.95 this would equate to 9500 IDR to 1 USD

Question 15: Parking Documents

What is document parking and why is it important when consideration internal control procedures and "segregation of duties" ?

A: Parking is a SAP term which means a posting (AP/AR/GL) can be temporarily saved (possibly with incomplete information) without hitting the affected ledger(s). A separate person can then release the posting to the ledger when required.

This is useful for example if junior staff are to initially enter the invoices, before their supervisor checks it and books it to the ledger.

Another popular use is when entering GL journals with many hundreds of line items. The document can be part-saved allowing for completion at a later date.

Question 16: Document Currency

Explain the document currency (WRBTR) and local currency fields (DMBTR) when posting a document in SAP FI.

A: On the document header, the currency key is entered. If this is different from the entity currency (or local currency), an equivalent amount in local currency is calculated automatically by the system and stored in the field "local currency". It is possible however to overwrite the system proposed value in this field manually.

If the local amount is manually overwritten, and the difference between the implied exchange rate is sufficiently different to the rate used by the system, a warning or error message is displayed (depending on system configuration)

Question 17: Substitution Rules

What are FI substitution rules ?

A: Defined in configuration they are similar to the FI validation rules above. Substitution rules allow field values to be replaced when certain pre-requisites conditions are met.

Question 18: Exchange Rate Types

What are exchange rate "types" in SAP ?

A: Exchange rate types are how SAP categorizes the different sets of exchange rates in the R'3 system.

By default exchange rate type "M" is used for the rates used to calculate local currency in the SAP system

ExRt	Usage
0011	Rate on key date
0012	Average rate
0013	Historical rate
0014	Rate on key date in previous year
0021	Rate on key date
0022	Average rate
0023	Historical rate
0024	Rate on key date in previous year

Question 19: Calculated Rate v Header Rate

During document postings, under what circumstances would SAP display the following warning / error message: "Calculated rate deviates from document header rate by x%"

A: This occurs when the exchange rate in the document header (either entered by the user or derived from the exchange rate table) differs by a larger amount than that specified as the maximum tolerance.

(The message can changed to be either an error or a warning)

Question 20: Foreign Currency

When entering foreign currency FI transactions describe the various ways in which the exchange rate is derived by SAP

A: The exchange rate can be entered via either:-

- Directly on the document header
- Derived from the exchange rate table (by leaving exchange rate blank)
- Indirectly, by entering the explicit local currency amount so the system is forced to use a specific exchange rate

Question 21: FB50 vs. FB01

What is the difference between the Enjoy SAP document entry screens (e.g. FB50, FB60 etc) and the old general posting transaction (FB01)

A: The Enjoy SAP screens were created to expedite data entry for AP,AR and GL postings.

In the old FB01 screen users were required to enter document types and posting keys manually to determine the nature of the postings. In the Enjoy SAP data entry screens these are defaulted via a configuration table so the user just has to choose debit/credit and the system will default the posting key. The document type is determined based on whether the entry is a vendor/customer invoice/credit memo or GL journal.

Question 22: Validation Rules

What are FI validation rules ?

A: Validation rules (configured via transaction OB28) enforce certain conditions when FI postings are made.

Validation rules comprise:-

- A prerequisite event that has to occur for the validation check to take place
- The check itself
- The output message that is to be displayed (you can choose between a warning or error message)

For example you may wish to ensure that users only enter GL journals with document type 'SA' for a specific GL account 88510005 in company code A100. Your prerequisite would be if the GL account = 88510005 and company code = A100. The check would be that the document type = SA and in the event of an incorrect entry the message could be "Error – only document type SA allowed"

You can enrich validation routines using ABAP code

Question 23: Internal Number Assignment

Explain the terms "internal number assignment" and "external number assignment" and the differences between them ? Why is it generally not a good idea to have external numbering on transactions ?

A: "Internal" numbering means the R/3 system assigns the next available sequential number to the master data object or transaction posting. "External" means the user has to manually enter the number during the creation of the master record or the posting of the document.

Entering the document number manually on each SAP financial posting is a time consuming effort and causes a risk to those transactions booked via interfaces. Often organizations want to do this to match source or legacy systems data with R/3. However there are plenty of text and reference fields available to store this information without requiring external numbering.

Part IV: General Ledger

Question 24: Transporting Tax Codes

Explain the procedure for transporting tax codes and their associated rates between SAP systems

A: Rather than simply attaching tax codes to a transport as per any other SAP configuration, a unique import/export routine needs to be followed which imports the settings into your productive SAP system

The export routine can be found under within IMG transaction FTXP via transport > tax code > export / import

The tax codes themselves have to be manually created in the target system. You leave the tax rates blank (your basis colleagues have to ensure your production system is open for configuration) and run the import routine. Note that the tax accounts have to be maintained manually in production also.

This is a common interview question which can be quickly used to test those with previous FI/CO experience.

Question 25: GR/IR Clearing

Explain what is meant by GR/IR clearing

A: Goods receipts from the MM module typically generate entries such as

- Debit Stock, Credit GR/IR clearing

This indicates an increase in stock and a pending entry to be cleared once the invoice from the vendor arrives.

At month end there will be a need to accrue those purchases received but not yet invoiced hence the reason for the account named 'Good Received / Invoice Received'

Typically the balance on this account at month end indicates the value of goods received but not invoiced.

Once the invoice is received the corresponding entry is booked.

- Credit Vendor, Debit GR/IR

These opposite entries to the GR/IR need to be cleared against each other. (This account is managed on an open item basis). Using the F.19 transaction this can be done automatically by using the PO and line item number stored in the assignment field

Question 26: Account Type Field

Explain the purpose of the account type field in the GL master record

A: At year end P&L accounts are cleared down to the retained earnings balance sheet account. This field contains an indicator which is linked (in the IMG transaction OB53) to the specific GL account use in this clear down.

Question 27: Alternative Account

What is the alternative account field used for in the GL master record ?

A: Another very popular interview question. This field can be used to store the old legacy system's account number against the new number in SAP.

A standard search help exists which will allow users to search for the SAP account based on the old legacy account number. This is particularly useful for new SAP users who are still getting used to the new chart of accounts.

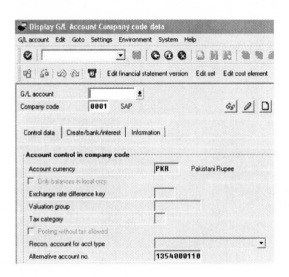

Question 28: GL Views

What is the difference between the chart of account view and company code view when maintaining a GL account ?

A: There are two screens which have to be maintained for each new GL account. The first is at 'chart of account' level (transaction FSPo) and contains the information used by all company codes using this chart of accounts such as description, group account number etc.

Each company code using this chart will then add its own company code view (via transaction code FSSo) which contains localized data specific to that entity e.g. field status group, alternative account number etc.

The chart of accounts screen must be maintained before the local company code screens.

Question 29: Sort Key

What is a sort key and what is it used for?

A: Sort keys are stored in customer, vendor and GL master records. They determine what value is populated in the 'assignment' field in the document line items posted.

There are several standard entries in a pre-delivered SAP system and additional entries can be configured if required.

A very common use for sort key 014 Purchase Order number for example, is to allow the GR/IR clearing GL account to be cleared automatically.

For FI/CO jobs in a logistics environment this is a common question.

Question 30: Fiscal Year Variant

What are fiscal year variants and how are fiscal periods opened and closed ?

A: Fiscal year variants (FSV's) are assigned to a company code via transaction OBY6. They determine the financial reporting periods of an entity e.g. 13 4-weekly periods, calendar months, 5-5-4 reporting etc

During month end the current fiscal reporting period will be and the next month opened. Its possible to open and close specific ledgers e.g. AP, AR, GL and even sets of accounts within those ledgers. This way its possible to, for example, close all GL accounts and leave only the month end adjustment accounts open for posting

Question 31: Special Periods

What are the special periods 13,14,15,16 and what are they used for ?

A: When you define the fiscal year variant you can choose to define additional special periods. These can be used for example for the posting of year end adjustments, auditors adjustments etc.

Periods 1-12 can be closed and periods 13-16 left open during year end closing

Question 32: GL Status Groups

What are GL field status groups and where are they used ?

A: Field status groups are defined in configuration and
are used to determine which fields are available for posting
when entries are booked against GL accounts.

Each field can be set as optional, mandatory or suppressed.

Field status variant AP01   Group SC01

General Posting

Additional account assignments

	Suppress	Req. entry	Opt. entry
Settlement period	O	O	⦿
Material number	⦿	O	O
Cost center	O	O	⦿
CO/PP order	O	O	⦿
WBS element	⦿	O	O
Sales order	⦿	O	O
Personnel number	O	O	⦿
Network	⦿	O	O
Commitment item	⦿	O	O
Plant	⦿	O	O
Business area	⦿	O	O
Trading partner business area	O	O	⦿
Quantity	⦿	O	O
Profit center	⦿	O	O
Profitability segment	⦿	O	O
Cost object	O	O	⦿
Joint venture acct assignment	⦿	O	O

Question 33: Recurring Entries

What are recurring entries and why are they used?

A: Recurring entries (setup in FBD1) can eliminate the need for the manual posting of accounting documents which do not change from month to month.

For example, a regular rental expense document can be created which can be scheduled for the last day of each month. Usually multiple recurring entries are created together and then processed as a batch at month end using transaction F.14

Question 34: Currency Revaluation

Explain how foreign currency revaluation works in SAP R/3 FI

A: Over time the local currency equivalent of foreign currency amounts will fluctuate according to exchange rate movements. Usually at month end, there is a requirement to restate these amounts using the prevailing month end exchange rates.

SAP can revalue foreign currency GL account balances as well as outstanding customer and vendor open item balances.

In SAP configuration, you define the balance sheet adjustment account and which accounts the realized gain/loss should be booked.

A batch input session is created to automatically post the required adjustments.

Question 35: Account Clearing

During GL account clearing how can small differences be dealt with ?

A: During configuration a tolerance limit is set which defines the maximum differences allowed during clearing.

The differences can be automatically booked by the system to a specific account during posting (using IMG transaction OBXZ)

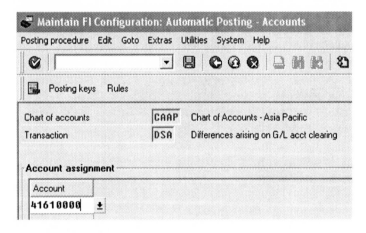

Part V: Controlling (CO)

Question 36: Disposing Assets

Describe three ways of disposing of an asset from a company code in SAP R/3

A: An existing asset can be scrapped (transaction ABAVN), transferred to another company code (ABUMN), sold to a customer account in the accounts receivable module (F-92), sold with revenue but the revenue is booked to a GL account (ABAON).

Question 37: Account Assignment Models

What are account assignment models ?

A: AAM's are blocks of document line items that can be used repeatedly to prevent manual re-entry.

Which fields are included in the AAM layout can be configured using O7E3

Question 38: CO-PCA

In Profit Center Accounting (CO-PCA) explain the process for locking planning data

A: Using transaction S_ALR_87004395, you can lock plan data for a specific fiscal year

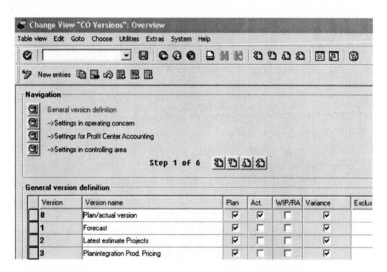

Select version 0 and choose 'settings for profit center accounting'.

Note the interviewer will not expect you to remember the transaction code but will expect you to refer to 'versions' and the fact that the plan can be locked per fiscal year and independently of the actual data.

Question 39: Value Field

What is a "value field" in the CO-PA module ?

A: Value fields are number/value related fields in profitability analysis such as quantity, sales revenue, discount value etc

Question 40: Characteristic Field

What is a "characteristic field" in the CO-PA module ?

A: Characteristics are analytical information fields used in CO-PA. Typical examples include customer number, brand, distribution channel etc

Question 41: COPA Basis

What is the difference between "costing based" (CB) and "account based" (AB) CO-PA ?

A: This is an incredibly popular question for any positions with a COPA component.

The interviewer will be looking for some of the following:-

- AB can easily be reconciled with FI at account level through the use of cost elements. CB can only be reconciled at account group level (such as revenues, sales deductions etc) as values are stored in "value fields" as opposed to accounts
- In CB data is stored by posting periods and weeks. In AB storage is only by periods.
- In CB transactions can be stored in operating concern currency and company code currency. In AB transactions are stored in controlling area currency, company code currency and transaction currency
- In CB you can create cross controlling area evaluations or cross controlling area plans. In AB you cannot as the chart of accounts may differ.
- In CB the cost of good sales (COGS) are updated via material price valuations. Stock change values can be transferred to CB COPA during billing. Timing differences can occur if the goods issue and billing documents are in different posting periods. In AB the value posted in the stock change is posted simultaneously to COPA.

Question 42: Operating Concern

What is an operating concern and what is its relationship with a controlling area in CO ?

A: The operating concern is the main organizational unit in Profitability Analysis. It's structure depends on the configuration setup of characteristics and value fields.

It is assigned to a controlling area on a one to may basis i.e. one controlling area may be assigned to only one operating concern, one operating concern can be assigned to many controlling areas.

Question 43: Internal Orders

What are statistical internal orders?

A: Statistical real internal orders are dummy cost objects used for analysis and reporting purposes. They must be posted to in conjunction with a real cost object such as a cost center.

For example for employees we define statistical internal orders and for departments we define cost centers. Travel expense invoices can then be booked to specific cost centers but analysis can also be done at employee level by looking at the statistical orders.

Statistical internal orders cannot be settled.

Question 44: Settlement Receivers

Name some settlement receivers for CO Internal Orders

A: Typically CO Internal Order are settled to:-

- Other internal orders
- Fixed assets (including assets under constructions)
- GL Accounts
- Cost Centres

Question 45: Performance Issues

What are the performances issue to be in mind when configuring Profitability analysis (COPA) ?

A: Sometimes COPA reporting performance is severely affected by poor initial setup. Anyone involved in a full COPA project lifecycle in a retail or manufacturing environment will have come across such issues hence the reason the interviewer is asking the question. The most important thing

Question 46 : Internal Order Controls

Explain some of the controls setup during the configuration of Internal Order Types in the CO module.

A: The following settings are made during the configuration of order types (transaction KOT2_OPA)

- Number ranges assigned to the order master on creation
- Planning and budgeting profiles
- Status profiles
- Order layouts

Question 47: Assessment vs. Distribution

Explain the differences between 'Assessment' and 'Distribution' cost allocation cycles in the R'3 CO module.

A: Its easiest to demonstrate this by way of an example

Lets say we have three cost elements with the following amounts to be allocated:-

A Electricity $2000
B Water $3000
C Canteen Costs $4000

With assessment cycles the system groups all three together and summarizes the balance of 9000$ onto a separate cost element e.g. D in order to allocate the costs to a receiving cost centre. Hence your sender cost element is D in your CO reporting and not A,B,C

With distributions the costs are allocated from the original cost elements. Hence your senders are A,B,C.

Question 48: Reconciliation Ledger

What is the CO reconciliation ledger and when would you typically use it ?

A: The reconciliation ledger effectively highlights differences by account across the FI and CO modules. A report is produced by the RL program, identifying where transactions have been booked across entities in controlling that would impact the external reporting produced from the FI module.

The RL program can then either post automatic corrections or you can choose to post manual corrections based on the information in the RL report.

Question 49: Freeze Data

Explain how using the "freeze data" option in COPA can speed up reporting performance.

A: Often companies that use COPA have extremely large volumes of data and reports can take several minutes, even hours, to run.

The 'free report data' option can be selected and the report run overnight. This way re-running the report online during the working data will see huge performance benefits as the system simply has to display stored stored and not recalculate it "on-the-fly"

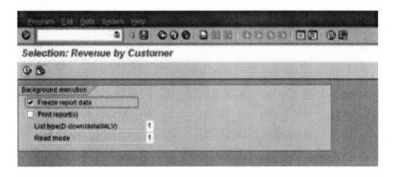

Questions regarding performance issues in COPA are common. You may be asked how summarization levels can increase reporting speed or alternatively asked to explain how you've minimized the number of characteristics with the same aim.

Question 50: Statistical Key Figures

What are statistical key figures in CO ?

A: SKF's are statistical (or information values) used in cost allocations such as assessments and distributions.

For example we may have an SKF for 'head count per department'. When utility costs are allocated across various departments we could perform the percentage allocation based on the 'head count' SKF.

Part VI: Fixed Assets (FA)

Question 51: Fixed asset reconciliation

How do you take the balances onto fixed asset reconciliation accounts during data take-on ?

A: Normally you cannot post direct to reconciliation accounts. However there is a configuration transaction OAK5/ OAMK which can be used to temporarily remove the reconciliation flags to allow the balances to be journal'ed onto the fixed asset reconciliation accounts.

Note this is a very popular interview question for FI/CO roles with FI-AA components.

Question 52: Acquisition Costs

Name three ways of posting acquisition cost to a fixed asset master

A: There are many ways of booking APC to fixed asset records including:-

- Via F-90 – Acquisition with Vendor
- ABZON – Acquisition with automatic offsetting entry
- ABZP – from affiliated company
- From settlement of an asset under construction (AIBU)
- From goods receipt (or invoice receipt depending on system setup) relating to a purchase order

Question 53: Sub assets

What are sub-assets and what would be a typical use for them in the SAP environment ?

A: Sub-assets are four digit reference numbers that are linked to the main asset number.

For example, if an asset 31000050 exists for a piece of machinery which initially cost $100,000 a sub-asset asset 0001 could be created and used to book additional cost (maybe a machinery upgrade) against the original asset. Both assets exist separately and can be reported as such or together.

When running the asset reports you can either run for the 31000050 asset or together with the sub asset 31000050-0001

If you have multiple sub-assets you can report based on 31000050-*

Using this approach asset components cost can be stored separately but reported together.

Note that these sub-assets are depreciated independently of their main asset – this is a popular interview question.

Question 54: Asset Under Construction

What is an "asset under construction"

A: AuC's can be used to track investment cost during projects or asset assembly. Following completion their costs can be settled to other fixed assets or to other CO cost objects such as real internal orders or cost centres.

For example, the construction of a new building, the various costs involved (engineering, utlity cost etc) could be collected under an AUC, before being settled to an asset under the "buildings' asset class at the end of the project.

AuC's generally are not depreciated until completion.

Question 55: Evaluation Groups

What are evaluation groups on the asset master used for ?

A: Allocation groups can be used to categorize assets whichever way the user chooses.

There are 4 with four characters (configured via OAVA transaction) and 1 with 8 characters (configured with OAV8). If you wish you can define a list of entries to be validated when the user populates these fields.

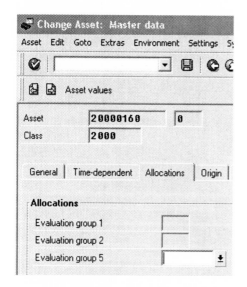

In customizing you can choose which of the 5 fields to display on the asset master record

Question 56: Fixed Asset Depreciation

What cost objects can be posted to automatically when the Fixed Asset Depreciation run is performed ?

A: In IMG transaction OAYR you can choose to allocate depreciation cost to :-

- Cost centers
- Internal Order
- Both of the above

The cost centers or order used is stored on the respective asset master record

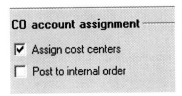

Question 57: Smoothing and Catchup

Explain the terms "smoothing" and "catchup" with regards fixed asset depreciation

A: This question refers to how SAP handles under/over depreciated assets with respect to future depreciation runs.

In IMG OAYR setting the smoothing flag forces the system to calculate depreciation evenly over the remaining periods in the fiscal year.

The opposite of this is with catch-up which means the system will correct any under/over depreciation in the next fiscal months depreciation run.

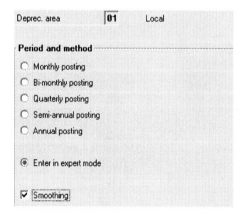

Part VI: Org Structure & Module Integration

Question 58: FI Global Settings

What is the difference between 'company code' and 'company ID' when in the FI global settings in the IMG?

A: The company code is the legal entity organization unit and the lowest level at which external financial statements are prepared.

The company id is a higher organization unit used for consolidation in the SAP system. A single company id can have many company codes assigned to it so long as the fiscal year variant and chart of accounts is consistent.

Question 59: Financial Statement

What is a 'financial statement version'?

A: Financial statement versions 'FSV's' are the structures forming the P'L and Balance sheet reports from the FI module.

Accounts are assigned to the end nodes in the reporting structure tree. Depending on the setup debit/credit balances can be reflected in different asset / liability columns where required

Question 60: New Company Code

How do you define a new company code ?

A: Using transaction code EC01, the most straightforward way of creating a new company code is to copy an existing value.

All associated data such as the fiscal year variant and assignments to controlling area and credit control area are taken across from the source value.

Transactional data of course is not copied.

Here, interviewers are simply looking to hear the word "copy" to prove that you have defined a SAP FI/CO organizational structure before.

Question 61: Chart of Accounts

If several chart of accounts are in use in a SAP system and there is a requirement to merge them to a single chart, how can this be achieved?

A: This is a little bit of a trick question. The interviewer here is checking your knowledge of modifying an existing organizational structure in an existing live SAP system.

Generally such changes cannot be done. The only options are:-

* Using specialist SAP consultants and their own ABAP tools to perform the conversion. This is a time consuming and expensive process
* Creating duplicate entities and transferring opening balances and year to data line items across.

The above applies for other such changes as modifying the local currency of an entity or merging several controlling areas.

You would be surprised how often interview candidates state "you would change the settings in configuration".

Questions such as these are not designed to deliberately send you down a blind alley but rather they act as a quick way to work out whether a candidate has simply dabbled around in the FI/CO modules or whether they have a

strong grasp of SAP organizational concepts in a live
environment

Question 62: What is stored in table T001 ?

A: This is the main company code configuration table and includes such assignments as:-

- Fiscal year variant
- Company assignment
- Local currency setting
- Credit control area

Question 63: Company Code

What is a company code ? Describe its relationship with a controlling area

A: A company code represents a specific legal entity for financial reporting purposes and represents the lowest level at which external financial accounts can be produced.

It's the main organizational object in the FI module and is assigned to a controlling area in CO. One company code may only be assigned to a single controlling area. (A controlling area may have multiple company codes assigned to it)

Question 64: SD and AR

Explain briefly how the Sales and Distribution modules creates Accounts Receivable line items for invoice postings.

A: Following the creation of a sales order, a goods issue is performed to issue the items out of stock. This typically generates the following FI entry:-

- Debit Cost of Sales, Credit Stock

Once the invoice (billing document) has been created in the SD module, the following entry is booked into the Accounts Receivable module

- Debit Customer, Credit Revenue

Using copy rules in SD, its possible to pass the sales order number or billing document number onto the AR posting for tracing and analysis purposes.

The above is a very basic example and can vary depending on the system setup however if you are being interviewed for a role with SD integration expect questions similar to the above.

Question 65: MM and AP

Explain briefly how the Materials Management module creates Accounts Payable line items for invoice postings.

A: Following the creation of a purchase order, a good receipt is booked to indicate the arrival of the stock from the vendor. This typically creates the following posting:-

- Debit Stock, Credit GR/IR clearing

Once the invoice is received from the vendor and booked in the invoice verification module in MM, an entry is created in the AP module

- Debit GR/IR Clearing, Credit Vendor

This is the classic MM to FI data flow and can vary on system setup. However for positions with integration to the logistics modules questions like this will almost inevitably pop up.

Question 66: Batch Input

Explain what 'batch input sessions' are, some examples of where they are used in FI/CO and the terms 'background' and 'foreground' processing.

A: Batch input sessions are batches of SAP data (either master data or transactional data) generated through an interface/report/bespoke user application.

For example when creating cost elements automatically using SAP transaction OKB2/OKB3 the system creates a batch session containing all the data required.

Batch input sessions are used extensively throughout the FI/CO modules including:-

- Depreciation run
- Recurring entries
- CO reconciliation ledger
- Master data creation in FI/CO
- FX revaluation

Foreground/background refers to how the users view the data being created by the SAP system. In foreground the user can step through each screen during data creation and correct any errors as they occur. In background the system tries to create the data for the entire batch and reports errors following completion.

Question 67: Commitment Line Items

What are 'commitment' line items in CO ?

A: Commitment line items in CO are not actual cost items but rather committed expenditure items generated through purchase orders.

They are flagged with a unique value type (e.g. 21 for Purchase Requisition Commitments and type 22 for Purchase Order Commitments) in the CO tables and can be reported separately in report painter

It's also possible to post manual commitment values in order to report non-PO related expenditure commitments.

Question 68: Special Purpose Ledger

When defining a new ledger in the Special Purpose ledger, how can you retrospectively populate FI data for a previous fiscal year ?

A: Using SAP transaction GCU1, FI data can be transferred for a particular company code, fiscal year or specific document number range.

A similar transaction exists for controlling data, GCU3.

Question 69: Using Special Purpose Ledger

What is the special purpose ledger and what would be some reasons for using it ?

A: The SPL is a user defined ledger which can be built to support reporting requirements which cannot normally be met through the usual SAP modules.

You can pull information from many SAP modules such as FI, CO, MM, SD and build user defined fields whose contents are based on calculations from other SAP standard information.

Typical uses include:-

- Reporting using an alternative fiscal year variant other than the one assigned to the entity.
- Reporting in a different currency (maybe to meet a new head office reporting currency)
- Meeting USGaap and local reporting requirements

Question 70: BSEG, BKPF, GLTO

Explain the purpose of the following SAP R/3 FI tables: BSEG, BKPF, GLTo

A: BKPF is the document header table. It stores all the fields common to all of the document line items such as posting date, currency key, document number etc

BSEG is the associated line item table to BKPF. Specific line item information such as posting key, GL account, document amount are stored.

GLTo is the summarized account balances table showing account balances by period, by account, by fiscal year.

Questions regarding tables may seem overly technical but interviews can quickly ascertain whether a potential candidate has worked in a pure end user role or in a hands on configuration role.

Question 71: COEP, CSKA, CE1XXXX

Explain the purpose of the following SAP R/3 CO tables: COEP, CSKA, CE1xxxx

A: COEP is the CO object line item table.

CSKA is the cost element master table (dependant on chart of accounts)

CE1xxxx (where xxxx is the name of your operating concern) is the profitability analysis line item table.

Question 72 : LSMW

What is the Legacy System Migration Workbench (LSMW) and when would you use it in your SAP FI/CO rollout ?

A: LSMW is a technical tool used for migrating master data and transaction data from your old 'legacy' systems to SAP.

Though usually setup by your ABAP programming colleagues, the LSMW projects are usually run by FI/CO project team members in order to upload vendors, customers, cost centers, internal orders etc

The interviewer is unlikely to ask any technically difficult questions but most experienced FI/CO team members who have been through a data migration stage will have at least a basic understanding of LSMW.

Question 73: Credit Checks

Describe some of the standard credit checks available within SAP. Where does most of the credit management information sit in the IMG ?

A: Credit management is one of the key integration areas between the Sales and Distribution modules (SD) and financial accounting (FI). Most of the configuration sits in the SD IMG menu under   Sales and Distribution > Basic Functions > Credit Management/Risk Management > Credit Management > Define Automatic Credit Control

The following are the standard credit checks available

- Static (a simple check against customers credit limits of the total AR open items, SD billing docs etc)
- Dynamic (as above but including open sales orders not yet delivered over a particular time period)
- Maximum sales order or delivery specified
- Critical field check (for such fields as payment terms)
- Next Review Date – checks the review date stored on the customer master
- AR open items – checks existing overdue items on the customer account
- Highest dunning level – specifies a max dunning level allowed

CCA	RkC	CG	Credit control		Curr.	Update
0001	001	01	High Risk Sales Orders		USD	000012

Document controlling

No credit check ☐

☐ Item check

Released documents are still unchecked

Deviation in % ☐

Number of days ☐

Credit limit seasonal factor

% Minus From To

☐ ☐ ☐

Checks in financial accounting/old A/R summary

☐ Payer

Permitted days ☐   Permitted hours ☐

Checks

```
                 Reaction Status/Block
```

		Reaction	Status/Block			
☑	Static		☐	☐ Open orders	☐ Open deliveries	
☑	Dynamic	A	☑	Horizon	2	M
☑	Document value	B	☐	Max. doc. value	9.999.999,00	
☑	Critical fields	A	☑			
☑	NextReview date	A	☑	Number of days		
☑	Open items	A	☑	Max. open. item %	50	NoDays openI
☐	OldestOpenItem	A	☑	Days oldestItem	100	
☑	High.dunn.level	A	☑	High.dunn.level	1	

Question 74: Report Painter

What is the report painter?

A: The report painter is a pre-delivered SAP reporting tool for the controlling module. It allows SAP reports to be quickly created, typically actual versus plan analysis for cost elements, internal orders and cost centers.

Question 75: User Exits

What are user exits and name an example where one could be used in the FI/CO modules

A: User exits are SAP supplied 'hooks' within specific program which allow user customizations to meet specific requirements.

When the program is run, SAP checks to see if the user has setup any logic within these hooks.

For example in the fixed asset module lets say the gain/loss from disposal is normally booked to GL account 65410. During posting however you wish to book certain asset retirement transaction types to 65499 for reporting purposes. An enhancement AINT0002 exists to do this.

User exits are commonly used also with validation and substitution rules.

To implement user exist you need an understanding of the ABAP programming language. However for those who have worked across several SAP projects its inevitable that at some point they will have come across user exits at some stage even if its just at a conceptual level.

Part II: Table & Transaction Code Reference

Table List

AGKO	Cleared Accounts
ANAR	Asset Types
ANAT	Asset type text
ANEK	Document Header Asset Posting
ANEP	Asset Line Items
ANEV	Asset downpymt settlement
ANKT	Asset classes- Description
ANLA	Asset Master Record Segment
ANLB	Depreciation terms
ANLC	Asset Value Fields
ANLH	Main asset number
AT02T	Transaction Activity Category - Description
AT02A	Transaction Code for Menu TIMN
AT10	Transaction type
AT10T	Name of Transaction Type
BKDF	Document Header Supplement for Recurring Entry
BKORM	Accounting Correspondence Requests
BKPF	Accounting Document Header
BLPK	Document log header
BLPP	Document log item
BLPR	Document Log Index and Planned Order (Backflush)
BNKA	Bank master record
BP000	Business Partner Master (General Data)
BPBK	Doc.Header Controlling Obj.
BPEG	Line Item Total Values Controlling Obj.
BPEJ	Line Item Annual Values Controlling Obj.
BPEP	Line Item Period Values Controlling Obj.
BPGE	Totals Record for Total Value Controlling obj.
BPJA	Totals Record for Annual Total Controlling Obj.

BSAD	Accounting- Secondary Index for Customers (Cleared Items)
BSAK	Accounting- Secondary Index for Vendors (Cleared Items)
BSAS	Accounting- Secondary Index for G/L Accounts (Cleared Items)
BSEC	One-Time Account Data Document Segment
BSEG	Accounting Document Segment
BSID	Accounting- Secondary Index for Customers
BSIK	Accounting- Secondary Index for Vendors
BSIM	Secondary Index, Documents for Material
BSIS	Accounting- Secondary Index for G/L Accounts
CEPC	Profit Center Master Data Table
CEPCT	Texts for Profit Center Master Data
COBRA	Settlement Rule for Order Settlement
COBRB	Distribution Rules Settlement Rule Order Settlement
COKA	CO Object- Control Data for Cost Elements
COSP	CO Object- Cost Totals for External Postings
COSS	CO Object- Cost Totals for Internal Postings
CRCO	Assignment of Work Center to Cost Center
CSKA	Cost Elements (Data Dependent on Chart of Accounts)
CSKB	Cost Elements (Data Dependent on Controlling Area)
CSLA	Activity master
FEBEP	Electronic Bank Statement Line Items
FPLA	Billing Plan
FPLT	Billing Plan- Dates
GLPCT	EC-PCA- Totals Table
KNA1	General Data in Customer Master
KOMK	Pricing Communication Header
MAHNV	Management Records for the Dunning Program
REGUT	TemSe - Administration Data
SKA1	G/L Account Master (Chart of Accounts)
SKAT	G/L Account Master Record (Chart of Accounts- Description)
SKB1	G/L account master (company code)

SAP FI/CO Interview Questions

T003T	Document Type Texts
T007S	Tax Code Names
T087J	Text
TAPRFT	Text tab. for investment profile
TKA01	Controlling Areas
TKA09	Basic Settings for Versions
TKVS	CO Versions
TZB0T	Flow types text table
TZPAT	Financial Assets Management product type texts
VBSEGS	Document Segment for G/L Accounts Document Parking
VTBFHA	Transaction
VTBFHAPO	Transaction Flow
VTBFHAZU	Transaction Activity
VTBFINKO	Transaction Condition
VTIDERI	Master Data Listed Options and Futures
VTIFHA	Underlying transaction
VTIFHAPO	Underlying transaction flows
VTIFHAZU	Underlying transaction status table
VTIOF	Options Additional Data
VWPANLA	Asset master for securities

Transaction Code List

F-01   Enter Sample Document
F-02   Enter G/L Account Posting
F-03   Clear G/L Account
F-04   Post with Clearing
F-05   Post Foreign Currency Valuation
F-06   Post Incoming Payments
F-07   Post Outgoing Payments
F-18   Payment with Printout
F-19   Reverse Statistical Posting
F-20   Reverse Bill Liability
F-21   Enter Transfer Posting
F-22   Enter Customer Invoice
F-23   Return Bill of Exchange Pmt Request
F-25   Reverse Check/Bill of Exch.
F-26   Incoming Payments Fast Entry
F-27   Enter Customer Credit Memo
F-28   Post Incoming Payments
F-29   Post Customer Down Payment
F-30   Post with Clearing
F-31   Post Outgoing Payments
F-32   Clear Customer
F-33   Post Bill of Exchange Usage
F-34   Post Collection
F-35   Post Forfaiting
F-36   Bill of Exchange Payment
F-37   Customer Down Payment Request
F-38   Enter Statistical Posting
F-39   Clear Customer Down Payment
F-40   Bill of Exchange Payment
F-41   Enter Vendor Credit Memo
F-42   Enter Transfer Posting
F-43   Enter Vendor Invoice
F-44   Clear Vendor
F-46   Reverse Refinancing Acceptance
F-47   Down Payment Request
F-48   Post Vendor Down Payment
F-49   Customer Noted Item
F-51   Post with Clearing
F-52   Post Incoming Payments
F-53   Post Outgoing Payments

F-54	Clear Vendor Down Payment
F-55	Enter Statistical Posting
F-56	Reverse Statistical Posting
F-57	Vendor Noted Item
F-58	Payment with Printout
F-59	Payment Request
F-60	Maintain Table: Posting Periods
F-62	Maintain Table: Exchange Rates
F-63	Park Vendor Invoice
F-64	Park Customer Invoice
F-65	Preliminary Posting
F-66	Park Vendor Credit Memo
F-67	Park Customer Credit Memo
F-90	Acquisition from purchase w. vendor
F-91	Asset acquis. to clearing account
F-92	Asset Retire. frm Sale w/ Customer
F.01	ABAP/4 Report: Balance Sheet
F.02	Compact Journal
F.03	Reconciliation
F.04	G/L: Create Foreign Trade Report
F.05	Foreign Currency Val.: Open Items
F.06	Foreign Currency Valuation:G/L Assts
F.07	G/L: Balance Carried Forward
F.08	G/L: Account Balances
F.09	G/L: Account List
F.0A	G/L: FTR Report on Disk
F.0B	G/L: Create Z2 to Z4
F.10	G/L: Chart of Accounts
F.11	G/L: General Ledger from Doc.File
F.12	Advance Tax Return
F.13	ABAP/4 Report: Automatic Clearing
F.14	ABAP/4 Report: Recurring Entries
F.15	ABAP/4 Report: List Recurr.Entries
F.16	ABAP/4 Report: G/L Bal.Carried Fwd
F.17	ABAP/4 Report: Cust.Bal.Confirmation
F.18	ABAP/4 Report: Vend.Bal.Confirmation
F.19	G/L: Goods/Invoice Received Clearing
F.1A	Customer/Vendor Statistics
F.1B	Head Office and Branch Index
F.20	A/R: Account List
F.21	A/R: Open Items
F.22	A/R: Open Item Sorted List
F.23	A/R: Account Balances
F.24	A/R: Interest for Days Overdue

SAP FI/CO Interview Questions

F.25   Bill of Exchange List
F.26   A/R: Balance Interest Calculation
F.27   A/R: Periodic Account Statements
F.28   Customers: Reset Credit Limit
F.29   A/R: Set Up Info System 1
F.2A   Calc.cust.int.on arr.: Post (w/o OI)
F.2B   Calc.cust.int.on arr.: Post(with OI)
F.2C   Calc.cust.int.on arr.: w/o postings
F.2D   Customrs: FI-SD mast.data comparison
F.2E   Reconciliation Btwn Affiliated Comps
F.2F   Management Acct Group Reconciliation
F.2G   Create Account Group Reconcil. G/L
F.30   A/R: Evaluate Info System
F.31   Credit Management - Overview
F.32   Credit Management - Missing Data
F.33   Credit Management - Brief Overview
F.34   Credit Management - Mass Change
F.35   Credit Master Sheet
F.36   Adv.Ret.on Sls/Pur.Form Printout(DE)
F.37   Adv.rept.tx sls/purch.form print (BE
F.38   Transfer Posting of Deferred Tax
F.39   C FI Maint. table To42Z (BillExcTyp)
F.40   A/P: Account List
F.41   A/P: Open Items
F.42   A/P: Account Balances
F.44   A/P: Balance Interest Calculation
F.45   A/P: Set Up Info System 1
F.46   A/P: Evaluate Info System
F.47   Vendors: calc.of interest on arrears
F.48   Vendors: FI-MM mast.data comparison
F.4A   Calc.vend.int.on arr.: Post (w/o OI)
F.4B   Calc.vend.int.on arr.: Post(with OI)
F.4C   Calc.vend.int.on arr.: w/o postings
F.50   G/L: Profitability Segment Adjustmnt
F.51   G/L: Open Items
F.52   G/L: Acct Bal.Interest Calculation
F.53   G/L: Account Assignment Manual
F.54   G/L: Structured Account Balances
F.56   Delete Recurring Document
F.57   G/L: Delete Sample Documents
F.58   OI Bal.Audit Trail: fr.Document File
F.59   Accum.Clas.Aud.Trail: Create Extract
F.5A   Accum.Clas.Aud.Trail: Eval.Extract
F.5B   Accum.OI Aud.Trail: Create Extract

F.5C   Accum.OI Audit Trail: Display Extr.
F.5D   G/L: Update Bal. Sheet Adjustment
F.5E   G/L: Post Balance Sheet Adjustment
F.5F   G/L: Balance Sheet Adjustment Log
F.5G   G/L: Subseq.Adjustment(BA/PC) Sp.ErA
F.5I   G/L: Adv.Rep.f.Tx on Sls/Purch.w.Jur
F.61   Correspondence: Print Requests
F.62   Correspondence: Print Int.Documents
F.63   Correspondence: Delete Requests
F.64   Correspondence: Maintain Requests
F.65   Correspondence: Print Letters (Cust)
F.66   Correspondence: Print Letters (Vend)
F.70   Bill/Exchange Pmnt Request Dunning
F.71   DME with Disk: B/Excha. Presentation
F.75   Extended Bill/Exchange Information
F.77   C FI Maintain Table T045D
F.78   C FI Maintain Table T045B
F.79   C FI Maintain Table T045G
F.80   Mass Reversal of Documents
F.81   Reverse Posting for Accr./Defer.Docs
F.90   C FI Maintain Table T045F
F.91   C FI Maintain Table T045L
F.92   C FI Maintain T012K (Bill/Exch.)
F.93   Maintain Bill Liability and Rem.Risk
F.97   General Ledger: Report Selection
F.98   Vendors: Report Selection
F.99   Customers: Report Selection
F/LA   Create Pricing Report
F/LB   Change pricing reports
F/LC   Display pricing reports
F/LD   Execute pricing reports
F00   SAPoffice: Short Message
F000   Accounting
F010   ABAP/4 Reporting: Fiscal Year Change
F01N   Debit position RA single reversal
F01O   Vacancy RU single reversal
F01P   Accruals/deferrals single reversal
F01Q   Debit position MC single reversal
F01R   MC settlement single reversal
F01S   Reverse Periodic Posting
F01T   Reverse Acc./Def. General Contract
F040   Reorganization
F041   Bank Master Data Archiving
F042   G/L Accounts Archiving

F043	Customer Archiving
F044	Vendor Archiving
F045	Document Archiving
F046	Transaction Figures Archiving
F101	ABAP/4 Reporting: Balance Sheet Adj.
F103	ABAP/4 Reporting: Transfer Receivbls
F104	ABAP/4 Reporting: Receivbls Provisn
F107	FI Valuation Run
F110	Parameters for Automatic Payment
F111	Parameters for Payment of PRequest
F13E	ABAP/4 Report: Automatic Clearing
F150	Dunning Run
F48A	Document Archiving
F53A	Archiving of G/L Accounts
F53V	Management of G/L Account Archives
F56A	Customer Archiving
F58A	Archiving of Vendors
F61A	Bank archiving
F64A	Transaction Figure Archiving
F66A	Archiving of Bank Data Storage
F8+0	Display FI Main Role Definition
F8+1	Maintain FI Main Role Definition
F8+2	Display FI Amount Groups
F8+3	Maintain FI Amount Groups
F8B4	C FI Maintain Table TBKDC
F8B6N	C FI Maintain Table TBKPV
F8BC	C FI Maintain Table TBKFK
F8BF	C FI Maintain Table T042Y
F8BG	Maintain Global Data for F111
F8BH	Inconsistencies T042I and T042Y
F8BJ	Maintain Clearing Accts (Rec.Bank)
F8BK	Maintain ALE-Compatible Pmnt Methods
F8BM	Maintain numb.range: Payment request
F8BN	Corr.Acctg Documents Payment Block
F8BO	Payment request archiving
F8BR	Levels for Payment Requests
F8BS	Detail display of payment requests
F8BT	Display Payment Requests
F8BU	Create payment runs automatically
F8BV	Reversal of Bank-to-Bank Transfers
F8BW	Reset Cleared Items: Payt Requests
F8BZ	F111 Customizing
F8XX	Payment Request No. Ranges KI3 -F8BM
FA39	Call up report with report variant

FAKA   Config.: Show Display Format
FAKP   Config.: Maintain Display Format
FAR1   S FI-ARI Maint. table T061A
FARA   S FI-ARI Maint. table T061P/Q
FARB   C FI-ARI Maint. table T061R
FARI   AR Interface: Third-party applicatns
FARY   Table T061S
FARZ   Table T061V
FAX1   BC sample SAP DE 2.1
FAX2   BC sample 2 SAP DE 2.1
FB00   Accounting Editing Options
FB01   Post Document
FB02   Change Document
FB03   Display Document
FB03Z Display Document/Payment Usage
FB04   Document Changes
FB05   Post with Clearing
FB05_OLD Post with clearing
FB07   Control Totals
FB08   Reverse Document
FB09   Change Line Items
FB10   Invoice/Credit Fast Entry
FB11   Post Held Document
FB12   Request from Correspondence
FB13   Release for Payments
FB1D   Clear Customer
FB1K   Clear Vendor
FB1S   Clear G/L Account
FB21   Enter Statistical Posting
FB22   Reverse Statistical Posting
FB31   Enter Noted Item
FB41   Post Tax Payable
FB50   G/L Acct Pstg: Single Screen Trans.
FB60   Enter Incoming Invoices
FB65   Enter Incoming Credit Memos
FB70   Enter Outgoing Invoices
FB75   Enter Outgoing Credit Memos
FB99   Check if Documents can be Archived
FBA1   Customer Down Payment Request
FBA2   Post Customer Down Payment
FBA3   Clear Customer Down Payment
FBA6   Vendor Down Payment Request
FBA7   Post Vendor Down Payment
FBA7_OLD Post Vendor Down Payment

FBA8   Clear Vendor Down Payment
FBA8_OLD Clear Vendor Down Payment
FBB1   Post Foreign Currency Valn
FBBA   Display Acct Determination Config.
FBBP   Maintain Acct Determination Config.
FBCJ   Cash Journal
FBCJC0   C FI Maintain Tables TCJ_C_JOURNALS
FBCJC1   Cash Journal Document Number Range
FBCJC2   C FI Maint. Tables TCJ_TRANSACTIONS
FBCJC3   C FI Maintain Tables TCJ_PRINT
FBCOPY   Copy Function Module
FBD1   Enter Recurring Entry
FBD2   Change Recurring Entry
FBD3   Display Recurring Entry
FBD4   Display Recurring Entry Changes
FBD5   Realize Recurring Entry
FBD9   Enter Recurring Entry
FBDF   Menu Banque de France
FBE1   Create Payment Advice
FBE2   Change Payment Advice
FBE3   Display Payment Advice
FBE6   Delete Payment Advice
FBE7   Add to Payment Advice Account
FBF1   C80 Reporting Minus Sp.G/L Ind.
FBF2   Financial Transactions
FBF3   Control Report
FBF4   Download Documents
FBF5   Reports Minus Vendor Accounts
FBF6   Document Changes
FBF7   C80 Reports Minus Sp.G/L Ind.
FBF8   C84 Reports
FBFT   Customizing BDF
FBIPU   Maintain bank chains for partner
FBKA   Display Accounting Configuration
FBKF   FBKP/Carry Out Function (Internal)
FBKP   Maintain Accounting Configuration
FBL1   Display Vendor Line Items
FBL1N   Vendor Line Items
FBL2   Change Vendor Line Items
FBL2N   Vendor Line Items
FBL3   Display G/L Account Line Items
FBL3N   G/L Account Line Items
FBL4   Change G/L Account Line Items
FBL4N   G/L Account Line Items

FBL5	Display Customer Line Items
FBL5N	Customer Line Items
FBL6	Change Customer Line Items
FBL6N	Customer Line Items
FBM1	Enter Sample Document
FBM2	Change Sample Document
FBM3	Display Sample Document
FBM4	Display Sample Document Changes
FBMA	Display Dunning Procedure
FBME	Banks
FBMP	Maintain Dunning Procedure
FBN1	Accounting Document Number Ranges
FBN2	Number Range Maintenance: FI_PYORD
FBP1	Enter Payment Request
FBR1	Post with Reference Document
FBR2	Post Document
FBRA	Reset Cleared Items
FBRC	Reset Cleared Items (Payment Cards)
FBS1	Enter Accrual/Deferral Doc.
FBTA	Display Text Determin.Configuration
FBTP	Maintain Text Determin.Configuration
FBU2	Change Intercompany Document
FBU3	Display Intercompany Document
FBU8	Reverse Cross-Company Code Document
FBV0	Post Parked Document
FBV1	Park Document
FBV2	Change Parked Document
FBV3	Display Parked Document
FBV4	Change Parked Document (Header)
FBV5	Document Changes of Parked Documents
FBV6	Parked Document $
FBVB	Post Parked Document
FBW1	Enter Bill of Exchange Pmnt Request
FBW2	Post Bill of Exch.acc.to Pmt Request
FBW3	Post Bill of Exchange Usage
FBW4	Reverse Bill Liability
FBW5	Customer Check/Bill of Exchange
FBW6	Vendor Check/Bill of Exchange
FBW7	Bank file to file system (for FBWD)
FBW8	File to Bank (for Transaction FBWD)
FBW9	C FI Maintain Table T045DTA
FBWA	C FI Maintain Table T046a
FBWD	Returned Bills of Exchange Payable
FBWD2	Parameter Transaction for FBWD

FBWE   Bill/Exch.Presentatn - International
FBWQ   C FI Maintain Table T045T
FBWR   C FI Maintain Table T045W
FBWS   C FI Maintain Table T046s
FBZo   Display/Edit Payment Proposal
FBZ1   Post Incoming Payments
FBZ2   Post Outgoing Payments
FBZ3   Incoming Payments Fast Entry
FBZ4   Payment with Printout
FBZ5   Print Check For Payment Document
FBZ8   Display Payment Run
FBZA   Display Pmnt Program Configuration
FBZG   Failed Customer Payments
FBZP   Maintain Pmnt Program Configuration
FC1o   Financial Statements Comparison
FC11   Data Extract for FI Transfer
FC8o   Document C80
FC82   Document C82
FCAA   Check Archiving
FCC1   Payment Cards: Settlement
FCC2   Payment Cards: Repeat Settlement
FCC3   Payment Cards: Delete Logs
FCC4   Payment Cards: Display Logs
FCCR   Payment Card Evaluations
FCH1   Display Check Information
FCH2   Display Payment Document Checks
FCH3   Void Checks
FCH4   Renumber Checks
FCH5   Create Check Information
FCH6   Change Check Information/Cash Check
FCH7   Reprint Check
FCH8   Reverse Check Payment
FCH9   Void Issued Check
FCHA   Check archiving
FCHB   Check retrieval
FCHD   Delete Payment Run Check Information
FCHE   Delete Voided Checks
FCHF   Delete Manual Checks
FCHG   Delete cashing/extract data
FCHI   Check Lots
FCHK   Check Tracing Initial Menu
FCHN   Check Register
FCHR   Online Cashed Checks
FCHT   Change check/payment allocation

FCHU   Create Reference for Check
FCHV   C FI Maintain Table TVOID
FCHX   Check Extract - Creation
FCIWCU BW Customizing for CS
FCIWD00 Download InfoObject text
FCIWD10 Download InfoObject hierarchies
FCKR   International cashed checks
FCMM   C FI Preparations for consolidation
FCMN   FI Initial Consolidation Menu
FCV1   Create A/R Summary
FCV2   Delete A/R Summary
FCV3   Early Warning List
FC_BW_BEX   Business Explorer Analyser
FC_BW_RSA1   BW Administrator Workbench
FC_BW_RSZDELETE Delete BW Query Objects
FC_BW_RSZV   Maintain BW Variables
FD-1   Number range maintenance: FVVD_RANL
FD01   Create Customer (Accounting)
FD02   Change Customer (Accounting)
FD02CORE Maintain customer
FD03   Display Customer (Accounting)
FD04   Customer Changes (Accounting)
FD05   Block Customer (Accounting)
FD06   Mark Customer for Deletion (Acctng)
FD08   Confirm Customer Individually(Actng)
FD09   Confirm Customer List (Accounting)
FD10   Customer Account Balance
FD10N   Customer Balance Display
FD10NA Customer Bal. Display with Worklist
FD11   Customer Account Analysis
FD15   Transfer customer changes: send
FD16   Transfer customer changes: receive
FD24   Credit Limit Changes
FD32   Change Customer Credit Management
FD33   Display Customer Credit Management
FD37   Credit Management Mass Change
FDCU   Loans customizing menu
FDFD   Cash Management Implementation Tool
FDI0   Execute Report
FDI1   Create Report
FDI2   Change Report
FDI3   Display Report
FDI4   Create Form
FDI5   Change Form

FDI6   Display Form
FDIB   Background Processing
FDIC   Maintain Currency Translation Type
FDIK   Maintain Key Figures
FDIM   Report Monitor
FDIO   Transport Reports
FDIP   Transport Forms
FDIQ   Import Reports from Client 000
FDIR   Import Forms from Client 000
FDIT   Translation Tool - Drilldown Report
FDIV   Maintain Global Variable
FDIX   Reorganize Drilldown Reports
FDIY   Reorganize Report Data
FDIZ   Reorganize Forms
FDK43   Credit Management - Master Data List
FDMN
FDOO   Borrower's notes order overview
FDTA   TemSe/REGUT Data Administration
FDTT   Treasury Data Medium Administration
FEBA   Postprocess Electronic Bank Statmt
FEBC   Generate Multicash format
FEBMSG   Display Internet Messages
FEBOAS   Request Account Statement via OFX
FEBOFX   OFX Functions
FEBP   Post Electronic Bank Statement
FEBSTS   Search String Search Simulation
FESR   Importing of POR File (Switzerland)
FEUB   Adjust VIB EPP after EURO conversion
FEUI   Real Estate Implementation Guide
FF$3   Send planning data to central system
FF$4   Retrieve planning data
FF$5   Retrieve transmission results
FF$6   Check settings
FF$7   Check all external systems
FF$A   Maintain TR-CM subsystems
FF$B   Convert Planning Group
FF$C   Convert planning level
FF$D   Convert business areas
FF$L   Display transmission information
FF$S   Display transmission information
FF$X   Configure the central TR-CM system
FF-1   Outstanding Checks
FF-2   Outstanding Bills of Exchange
FF-3   Cash Management Summary Records

FF-4   CMF Data In Accounting Documents
FF-5   CMF Records fr.Materials Management
FF-6   CMF Records from Sales
FF-7   Forecast Item Journal
FF-8   Payment Advice Journal
FF-9   Journal
FF.1   Standard G/L Account Interest Scale
FF.3   G/L Account Cashed Checks
FF.4   Vendor Cashed Checks
FF.5   Import Electronic Bank Statement
FF.6   Display Electronic Bank Statement
FF.7   Payment Advice Comparison
FF.8   Print Payment Orders
FF.9   Post Payment Orders
FF.D   Generate payt req. from advices
FF/1   Compare Bank Terms
FF/2   Compare value date
FF/3   Archive advices from bank statements
FF/4   Import electronic check deposit list
FF/5   Post electronic check deposit list
FF/6   Deposit/loan mgmt analysis/posting
FF/7   Deposit/loan management int accruals
FF/8   Import Bank Statement into Cash Mgmt
FF/9   Compare Advices with Bank Statement
FF63   Create Planning Memo Record
FF65   List of Cash Management Memo Records
FF67   Manual Bank Statement
FF68   Manual Check Deposit Transaction
FF6A   Edit Cash Mgmt Pos Payment Advices
FF6B   Edit liquidity forecast planned item
FF70   Cash Mgmt Posit./Liquidity Forecast
FF71   Cash Position
FF72   Liquidity forecast
FF73   Cash Concentration
FF74   Use Program to Access Cash Concntn
FF7A   Cash Position
FF7B   Liquidity forecast
FF:1   Maintain exchange rates
FFB4   Import electronic check deposit list
FFB5   Post electronic check deposit list
FFL_OLD Display Transmission Information
FFS_OLD Display Transmission Information
FFTL   Telephone list
FFW1   Wire Authorization

FFWR   Post Payment Requests from Advice
FFWR_REQUESTS   Create Payment Requests from Advice
FF_1   Standard G/L Account Interest Scale
FF_3   G/L Account Cashed Checks
FF_4   Vendor Cashed Checks
FF_5   Import Electronic Bank Statement
FF_6   Display Electronic Bank Statement
FG99   Flexible G/L: Report Selection
FGI0   Execute Report
FGI1   Create Report
FGI2   Change Report
FGI3   Display Report
FGI4   Create Form
FGI5   Change Form
FGI6   Display Form
FGIB   Background Processing
FGIC   Maintain Currency Translation Type
FGIK   Maintain Key Figures
FGIM   Report Monitor
FGIO   Transport Reports
FGIP   Transport Forms
FGIQ   Import Reports from Client 000
FGIR   Import Forms from Client 000
FGIT   Translation Tool - Drilldown Report.
FGIV   Maintain Global Variable
FGIX   Reorganize Drilldown Reports
FGIY   Reorganize Report Data
FGIZ   Reorganize Forms
FGM0   Special Purpose Ledger Menu
FGRP   Report Painter
FGRW   Report Writer Menu
FI01   Create Bank
FI02   Change Bank
FI03   Display Bank
FI04   Display Bank Changes
FI06   Mark Bank for Deletion
FI07   Change Current Number Range Number
FI12   Change House Banks/Bank Accounts
FI12CORE   Change House Banks/Bank Accounts
FI13   Display House Banks/Bank Accounts
FIBB   Bank chain determination
FIBC   Scenarios for Bank Chain Determin.
FIBD   Allocation client
FIBF   Maintenance transaction BTE

FIBHS   Display bank chains for house banks
FIBHU   Maintain bank chains for house banks
FIBL1   Control Origin Indicator
FIBL2   Assign Origin
FIBL3   Group of House Bank Accounts
FIBPS   Display bank chians for partners
FIBPU   Maintain bank chains for partner
FIBTS   Dis. bank chains for acct carry over
FIBTU   Main. bank chains for acctCarry over
FIHC   Create Inhouse Cash Center
FILAUF_WF_CUST Store Order: Workflow Customizing
FILE   Cross-Client File Names/Paths
FILINV_WF_CUST Store Inventory:Workflow Customizing
FINA   Branch to Financial Accounting
FINF   Info System Events
FINP   Info System Processes
FITP_RESPO   Contact Partner Responsibilities
FITP_SETTINGS Settings for Travel Planning
FITP_SETTINGS_TREE   Tree Maintenance Current Settings
FITVFELD   Tree
FJA1   Inflation Adjustment of G/L Accounts
FJA2   Reset Transaction Data G/L Acc.Infl.
FJA3   Balance Sheet/P&L with Inflation
FJA4   Infl. Adjustment of Open Items (FC)
FJA5   Infl. Adj. of Open Receivables (LC)
FJA6   Infl. Adj. of Open Payables (LC)
FJEE   Exercise Subscription Right
FK01   Create Vendor (Accounting)
FK02   Change Vendor (Accounting)
FK02CORE   Maintain vendor
FK03   Display Vendor (Accounting)
FK04   Vendor Changes (Accounting)
FK05   Block Vendor (Accounting)
FK06   Mark Vendor for Deletion (Acctng)
FK08   Confirm Vendor Individually (Acctng)
FK09   Confirm Vendor List (Accou nting)
FK10   Vendor Account Balance
FK10N   Vendor Balance Display
FK10NA   Vendor Balance Display
FK15   Transfer vendor changes: receive
FK16   Transfer vendor changes: receive
FKI0   Execute Report
FKI1   Create Report
FKI2   Change Report

FKI3	Display Report
FKI4	Create Form
FKI5	Change Form
FKI6	Display Form
FKIB	Background Processing
FKIC	Maintain Currency Translation Type
FKIK	Maintain Key Figures
FKIM	Report Monitor
FKIO	Transport Reports
FKIP	Transport Forms
FKIQ	Import Reports from Client 000
FKIR	Import Forms from Client 000
FKIT	Translation Tool - Drilldown Report.
FKIV	Maintain Global Variable
FKIX	Reorganize Drilldown Reports
FKIY	Reorganize Report Data
FKIZ	Reorganize Forms
FKMN	
FKMT	FI Acct Assignment Model Management
FLB1	Postprocessing Lockbox Data
FLB2	Import Lockbox File
FLBP	Post Lockbox Data
FLCV	Create/Edit Document Template WF
FM+0	Display FM Main Role Definition
FM+1	Maintain FM Main Role Definition
FM+2	Display FM Amount Groups
FM+3	Maintain FM Amount Groups
FM+4	Display FM Budget Line Groups
FM+5	Maintain FM Budget Line Groups
FM+6	Display FM Document Classes
FM+7	Maintain FM Document Classes
FM+8	Display FM Activity Categories
FM+9	Maintain FM Activity Categories
FM+A	Display Doc.Class->Doc.Cat. Assgmt
FM+B	Maintain Doc.Clase->Doc.Cat.Assgmt
FM03	Display FM Document
FM21	Change Original Budget
FM22	Display Original Budget
FM25	Change Supplement
FM26	Display Supplement
FM27	Change Return
FM28	Transfer Budget
FM29	Display Return
FM2D	Display Funds Center Hierarchy

FM2E   Change Budget Document
FM2F   Display Budget Document
FM2G   Funds Center Hierarchy
FM2H   Maintain Funds Center Hierarchy
FM2I   Create Funds Center
FM2S   Display Funds Center
FM2T   Change Releases
FM2U   Change Funds Center
FM2V   Display Releases
FM3D   Display Commitment Item Hierarchy
FM3G   Commitment Item Hierarchy
FM3H   Maintain Commitment Item Hierarchy
FM3I   Create Commitment Item
FM3N   Commitment Items for G/L Accounts
FM3S   Display Commitment Item
FM3U   Change Commitment Item
FM48   Change Financial Budget: Initial Scn
FM48_1   PS-CM: Create Planning Layout
FM48_2   PS-CM: Change Planning Layout
FM48_3   PS-CM: Display Planning Layout
FM49   Display Financial Budget: Init.Scrn
FM4G   Budget Structure Element Hierarchy
FM5I   Create Fund
FM5S   Display Fund
FM5U   Change Fund
FM5_DEL   Delete fund preselection
FM5_DISP   Display fund preselection
FM5_SEL   Preselection Fund
FM6I   Create Application of Funds
FM6S   Display Application of Funds
FM6U   Change Application of Funds
FM71   Maintain Cover Pools
FM72   Assign FM Acct Asst to Cover Pool
FM78   Charact.Groups for Cover Pools
FM79   Grouping Chars for Cover Pool
FM7A   Display Cover Eligibility Rules
FM7I   Create Attributes for FM Acct Asst
FM7P   Maintain Cover Eligibility Rules
FM7S   Display Cover Eligibility Rules
FM7U   Maintain Cover Eligibility Rules
FM9B   Copy Budget Version
FM9C   Plan Data Transfer from CO
FM9D   Lock Budget Version
FM9E   Unlock Budget Version

FM9F   Delete Budget Version
FM9G   Roll Up Supplement
FM9H   Roll up Original Budget
FM9I   Roll Up Return
FM9J   Roll Up Releases
FM9K   Change Budget Structure
FM9L   Display Budget Structure
FM9M   Delete Budget Structure
FM9N   Generate Budget Object
FM9P   Reconstruct Budget Distrbtd Values
FM9Q   Total Up Budget
FM9W   Adjust Funds Management Budget
FMA1   Matching: Totals and Balances (CBM)
FMA2   Matching: CBM Line Items and Totals
FMA3   Matching: FI Line Items (CBM)
FMA4   Matching: FI Bank Line Items (CBM)
FMAA   Matching: Line Items and Totals (FM)
FMAB   Matching: FI FM Line Items
FMAC   Leveling: FM Commitment Line Items
FMAD   Leveling: FI-FM Totals Records
FMAE   Display Change Documents
FMAF   Level Line Items and Totals Items
FMB0   CO Document Transfer
FMB1   Display Security Prices-Collect.
FMBI   Use Revenues to Increase Expend.Bdgt
FMBUD005   FIFM Budget Data Export
FMBUD006   FIFM Budget Data Import
FMBV   Activate Availability Control
FMC2   Customizing in Day -to-Day Business
FMCB   Reassignment: Document Selection
FMCC   Reassignment: FM-CO Assignment
FMCD   Reassignment: Delete Work List
FMCG   Reassignment: Overall Assignment
FMCN   Reassignment: Supplement.Acct Assgt
FMCR   Reassignment: Display Work List
FMCT   Reassignment: Transfer
FMD1   Change Carryforward Rules
FMD2   Display Carryforward Rules
FMDM   Monitor Closing Operations
FMDS   Copy Carryforward Rules
FMDT   Display Carryforward Rules
FME1   Import Forms from Client 000
FME2   Import Reports from Client 000
FME3   Transport Forms

FME4   Transport Reports
FME5   Reorganize Forms
FME6   Reorganize Drilldown Reports
FME7   Reorganize Report Data
FME8   Maintain Batch Variants
FME9   Translation Tool - Drilldown
FMEB   Structure Report Backgrnd Pr ocessing
FMEH   SAP-EIS: Hierarchy Maintenance
FMEK   FMCA: Create Drilldown Report
FMEL   FMCA: Change Drilldown Report
FMEM   FMCA: Display Drilldown Report
FMEN   FMCA: Create Form
FMEO   FMCA: Change Form
FMEP   FMCA: Display Form
FMEQ   FMCA: Run Drilldown Report
FMER   FMCA: Drilldown Tool Test Monitor
FMEURO1 Create Euro FM Area
FMEURO2 Refresh Euro Master Data
FMEURO3 Display Euro FM Areas
FMEURO4 Deactivate Euro FM Areas
FMEV   Maintain Global Variable
FMF0   Payment Selection
FMF1   Revenue Transfer
FMG1   FM: Create Commitment Item Group
FMG2   FM: Change Commitment Item Group
FMG3   FM: Display Commitment Item Group
FMG4   FM: Delete Commitment Item Group
FMG5   Generate BS Objects fr.Cmmt Item Grp
FMHC   Check Bdgt Structure Elements in HR
FMHG   Generate Bdgt Struc Elements in HR
FMHGG   Generate BS Elements f. Several Fnds
FMHH   Master Data Check
FMHIST Apportion Document in FM
FMHV   Budget Memo Texts
FMIA   Display Rules for Revs.Incr.Budget
FMIB   Increase Budget by Revenues
FMIC   Generate Additional Budget Incr.Data
FMIL   Delete Rules for Revs Incr. Budget
FMIP   Maintain Rules for Revs.Incr.Budget
FMIS   Display Rules for Revs.Incr.Budget
FMIU   Maintain Rules for Revs.Incr.Budget
FMJ1   Fiscal Year Close: Select Commitment
FMJ1_TR Settlement: Select Commitment
FMJ2   Fiscal Year Close: Carr.Fwd Commts

FMJ2_TR Settlement: Transfer Commitment
FMJ3   Reverse Commitments Carryforward
FMJA   Budget Fiscal Year Close: Prepare
FMJA_TR Budget Settlement: Prepare
FMJB   Determine Budget Year-End Closing
FMJB_TR Budget Settlement: Determine
FMJC   Budget Fiscal-Year Close: Carry Fwd
FMJC_TR Budget Settlement: Transfer
FMJD   Reverse Fiscal Year Close: Budget
FMLD   Ledger Deletion
FMLF   Classify Movement Types
FMN0   Subsequent Posting of FI Documents
FMN1   Subsequent Posting of MM Documents
FMN2   Subsequent Posting of Billing Docs
FMN3   Transfer Purchase Req. Documents
FMN4   Transfer Purchase Order Documents
FMN5   Transfer Funds Reservation Documents
FMN8   Simulation Lists Debit Position
FMN8_OLD   Simulation Lists Debit Position
FMN9   Posted Debit Position List
FMN9_OLD   Posted Debit Position List
FMNA   Display CBA Rules
FMNP   Maintain CBA Rules
FMNR   Assign SN-BUSTL to CBA
FMNS   Display CBA Rules
FMNU   Maintain CBA Rules
FMP0   Maintain Financial Budget
FMP1   Display Financial Budget
FMP2   Delete Financial Budget Version
FMR0   Reconstruct Parked Documents
FMR1   Actual/Commitment Report
FMR2   Actual/Commitment per Company Code
FMR3   Plan/Actual/Commitment Report
FMR4   Plan/Commitment Report w.Hierarchy
FMR5A   12 Period Forecast: Actual and Plan
FMR6A   Three Period Display: Plan/Actual
FMRA   Access Report Tree
FMRB   Access Report Tree
FMRE_ARCH   Archive Earmarked Funds
FMRE_EWU01   Earmarked Funds: Euro Preprocessing
FMRE_EWU02   Earmarked Funds: Euro Postprocessing
FMRE_SERLK   Close Earmarked Funds
FMRP18   Clear Subsequent Postings
FMSS   Display Status Assignment

FMSU	Change Assigned Status
FMU0	Display Funds Reservation Doc.Types
FMU1	Maintain Funds Reservation Doc.Types
FMU2	Display Funds Reservtn Fld Variants
FMU3	Maintain Funds Resvtn Field Variants
FMU4	Display Funds Reservation Fld Groups
FMU5	Maintain Funds Reservatn Fld Groups
FMU6	Display Funds Reservtn Field Selctn
FMU7	Maintain Funds Resvtn Field Selctn
FMU8	Display Template Type for Fds Resvtn
FMU9	Maintain Template Type for Fds Resvn
FMUA	Dispay Fds Res.Template Type Fields
FMUB	Maintain Fds Res.Template Type Flds
FMUC	Display Funds Res. Reference Type
FMUD	Maintain Funds Res.Reference Type
FMUE	Display Funds Res.Ref.Type Fields
FMUF	Maintaine Fds Rsvtn Ref.Type Fields
FMUG	Display Reasons for Decision
FMUH	Maintain Reasons for Decisions
FMUI	Display Groups for Workflow Fields
FMUJ	Maintain Groups for Workflow Fields
FMUK	Display Fields in Groups for WF
FMUL	Maintain Fields in Groups for WF
FMUM	Display Field Selctn ->Variant/Group
FMUN	Display Field Seln->Variant/Group
FMUV	Funds Resvtn Field Status Var.Asst
FMV1	Create Forecast of Revenue
FMV2	Change Forecast of Revenue
FMV3	Display Forecast of Revenue
FMV4	Approve Forecast of Revenue
FMV5	Change FM Acct Asst in Fcst of Rev.
FMV6	Reduce Forecast of Revenue Manually
FMVI	Create Summarization Item
FMVO	Fund Balance Carryforward
FMVS	Display Summarization Item
FMVT	Carry Forward Fund Balance
FMVU	Change Summarization Item
FMW1	Create Funds Blocking
FMW2	Change Funds Blocking
FMW3	Display Funds Blocking
FMW4	Approve Funds Blocking
FMW5	Change FM Acct Asst in Funds Blkg
FMWA	Create Funds Transfer
FMWAZ	Payment Transfer

FMWB   Change Funds Transfer
FMWC   Display Funds Transfer
FMWD   Approve Funds Transfer
FMWE   Change FM Acct Asst in Funds Trsfr
FMX1   Create Funds Reservation
FMX2   Change Funds Reservation
FMX3   Display Funds Reservation
FMX4   Approve Funds Reservation
FMX5   Change FM Acct Asst in Funds Resvn
FMX6   Funds Reservation: Manual Reduction
FMY1   Create Funds Commitment
FMY2   Change Funds Commitment
FMY3   Display Funds Precommitment
FMY4   Approve Funds Precommitment
FMY5   Change FM AcctAsst in Funds Prcmmt
FMY6   Reduce Funds Precommitment Manually
FMZ1   Create Funds Commitment
FMZ2   Change Funds Commitment
FMZ3   Display Funds Commitment
FMZ4   Approve Funds Commitment
FMZ5   Change FM Acct Asst in Funds Commt
FMZ6   Reduce Funds Commitment Manually
FMZBVT Carry Forward Balance
FMZZ   Revalue Funds Commitments
FM_DL07   Delete Worklist
FM_DLFI   Deletes FI Documnts Transferred from
FM_DLFM   Deletes all FM Data (fast)
FM_DLOI   Deletes Cmmts Transferred from FM
FM_EURO_M   Parameter maintenance for euro conv.
FM_RC06   Reconcile FI Paymts-> FM Totals Itms
FM_RC07   Reconcile FI Paymts-> FM Line Items
FM_RC08   Reconcile FM Paymts -> FM Line Items
FM_RC11   Select Old Payments
FM_S123   GR/IR: Post OIs to FM Again
FM_S201   Post Payments on Account to FIFM
FM_SD07   Display Worklist
FN-1   No.range: FVVD_RANL (Loan number)
FN-4   Number range maintenance: FVVD_PNNR
FN-5   Number range maintenance: FVVD_SNBNR
FN-6   Number range maintenance: FVVD_RPNR
FN09   Create Borrower's Note Order
FN11   Change borrower's note order
FN12   Display borrower's note order
FN13   Delete borrower's note order

FN15   Create borrower's note contract
FN16   Change borrower's note contract
FN17   Display borrower's note contract
FN18   Payoff borrower's note contract
FN19   Reverse borrower's note contract
FN1A   Create other loan contract
FN1V   Create other loan contract
FN20   Create borrower's note offer
FN21   Change borrower's note offer
FN22   Display borrower's note offer
FN23   Delete borrower's note offer
FN24   Activate borrower's note offer
FN2A   Change other loan application
FN2V   Change other loan contract
FN30   Create policy interested party
FN31   Change policy interested party
FN32   Display policy interested party
FN33   Delete policy interested party
FN34   Policy interested party in applic.
FN35   Policy interested party in contract
FN37   Loan Reversal Chain
FN3A   Display other loan application
FN3V   Display other loan contract
FN40   Create other loan interested party
FN41   Change other loan interested party
FN42   Display other loan interested party
FN43   Delete other loan interested party
FN44   Other loan interest.party in applic.
FN45   Other loan interested prty in cntrct
FN4A   Delete other loan application
FN4V   Delete other loan contract
FN5A   Other loan application in contract
FN5V   Payoff other loan contract
FN61   Create collateral value
FN62   Change collateral value
FN63   Display collateral value
FN70   List 25
FN72   List 54
FN80   Enter manual debit position
FN81   Change manual debit position
FN82   Display manual debit position
FN83   Create waiver
FN84   Change waiver
FN85   Display waiver

FN86	Enter debit position depreciation
FN87	Change debit position depreciation
FN88	Display debit position depreciation
FN8A	Manual Entry: Unsched. Repayment
FN8B	Manual Entry: Other Bus. Operations
FN8C	Manual Entry: Charges
FN8D	Post Planned Records
FNA0	Policy application in contract
FNA1	Create mortgage application
FNA2	Change mortgage application
FNA3	Display mortgage application
FNA4	Complete mortgage application
FNA5	Mortgage application in contract
FNA6	Create policy application
FNA7	Change policy application
FNA8	Display policy application
FNA9	Delete policy application
FNAA	Reactivate deleted mortgage applic.
FNAB	Reactivate deleted mortg. int.party
FNAC	Reactivate deleted mortgage contract
FNAD	Reactivate deleted policy applicat.
FNAE	Reactivate deleted policy contract
FNAG	Reactivate deleted other loan applic
FNAH	Reactivate del. other loan int.party
FNAI	Reactivate deleted other loan cntrct
FNAK	Select file character
FNAL	Reactivate deleted BNL contract
FNAM	Reactivate deleted policy contract
FNASL	Loans: Account Analysis
FNB1	Transfer to a Loan
FNB2	Transfer from a Loan
FNB3	Document Reversal - Loans
FNB8	BAV Information
FNB9	BAV transfer
FNBD	Loans-Automatic bal.sheet transfer
FNBG	Guarantee charges list
FNBU	DARWIN- Loans accounting menu
FNCD	Transfer Customizing for Dunning
FNCW1	Maintain Standard Role
FNCW2	Transaction Release: Adjust Workflow
FNDD	Convert Dunning Data in Dunn.History
FNEN	Create Loan
FNENALG	Create General Loan
FNENHYP	Create Mortgage Loan

FNENPOL   Create Policy Loan
FNENSSD   Create Borrower's Note Loan
FNF1   Rollover: Create file
FNF2   Rollover: Change file
FNF3   Rollover: Display file
FNF4   Rollover: Fill file
FNF9   Rollover: Evaluations
FNFO   ISIS: Create file
FNFP   ISIS: Change file
FNFQ   ISIS: Display file
FNFR   ISIS: Fill file
FNFT   Rollover: File evaluation
FNFU   Rollover: Update file
FNG2   Total Loan Commitment
FNG3   Total Commitment
FNI0
FNI1   Create mortgage application
FNI2   Change mortgage application
FNI3   Display mortgage application
FNI4   Delete mortgage application
FNI5   Mortgage application t o offer
FNI6   Mortgage application in contract
FNIA   Create interested party
FNIB   Change interested party
FNIC   Display interested party
FNID   Delete interested party
FNIE   Reactivate interested party
FNIH   Decision -making
FNIJ   Create credit standing
FNIK   Change credit standing
FNIL   Display credit standing
FNIN   Create collateral value
FNIO   Change collateral value
FNIP   Display collateral value
FNK0   Multimillion Loan Display (GBA14)
FNK1   Loans to Managers (GBA15)
FNKO   Cond.types - Cond.groups allocation
FNL1   Rollover: Create Main File
FNL2   Rollover: Change Main File
FNL3   Rollover: Displ. Main File Structure
FNL4   New business
FNL5   New business
FNL6   New business
FNM1   Automatic Posting

FNM1S	Automatic Posting - Single
FNM2	Balance sheet transfer
FNM3	Loans reversal module
FNM4	Undisclosed assignment
FNM5	Automatic debit position simulation
FNM6	Post dunning charges/int.on arrears
FNM7	Loan reversal chain
FNMA	Partner data: Settings menu
FNMD	Submenu General Loans
FNME	Loans management menu
FNMEC	Loans Management Menu
FNMH	Loans management menu
FNMI	Loans information system
FNMO	Loans Menu Policy Loans
FNMP	Rollover
FNMS	Loans Menu Borrower's Notes
FNN4	Display general file
FNN5	Edit general file
FNN6	Display general main file
FNN7	Edit general main file
FNN8	Display general main file
FNN9	Edit general overall file
FNO1	Create Object
FNO2	Change Object
FNO3	Display Object
FNO5	Create collateral
FNO6	Change collateral
FNO7	Display collateral
FNO8	Create Objects from File
FNO9	Create Collateral from File
FNP0	Edit rollover manually
FNP4	Rollover: Display file
FNP5	Rollover: Edit File
FNP6	Rollover: Display main file
FNP7	Rollover: Edit main file
FNP8	Rollover: Display overall file
FNP9	Rollover: Edit overall file
FNQ2	New Business Statistics
FNQ3	Postprocessing IP rejection
FNQ4	Custom er Inc. Payment Postprocessing
FNQ5	Transact.type - Acct determinat.adj.
FNQ6	Compare Flow Type/Account Determin.
FNQ7	Generate flow type
FNQ8	Automatic Clearing for Overpayments

FNQ9	Int. adjustment run
FNQF	Swiss interest adjustment run
FNQG	Swiss special interest run
FNR0	Loans: Posting Journal
FNR6	Insur.prtfolio trends - NEW
FNR7	Totals and Balance List
FNR8	Account statement
FNR9	Planning list
FNRA	Other accruals/deferrals
FNRB	Memo record update
FNRC	Accruals/deferrals reset
FNRD	Display incoming payments
FNRE	Reverse incoming payments
FNRI	Portfolio Analysis Discount/Premium
FNRS	Reversal Accrual/Deferral
FNS1	Collateral number range
FNS4	Cust. list parameters for loan order
FNS6	Installation parameter lists
FNS7	Loan Portfolio Trend Customizing
FNSA	Foreign currency valuation
FNSB	Master data summary
FNSL	Balance reconciliation list
FNT0	Loan correspondence (Switzerland)
FNT1	Autom. deadline monitoring
FNT2	Copy text modules to client
FNUB	Treasury transfer
FNV0	Payoff policy contract
FNV1	Create mortgage contract
FNV2	Change mortgage contract
FNV3	Display mortgage contract
FNV4	Delete mortgage contract
FNV5	Payoff mortgage contract
FNV6	Create policy contract
FNV7	Change policy contract
FNV8	Display policy contract
FNV9	Delete policy contract
FNVA	Create paid off contracts
FNVCOMPRESSION	Loans: Document Data Summarization
FNVD	Disburse Contract
FNVI	Loans: General Overview
FNVM	Change Contract
FNVR	Reactivate Contract
FNVS	Display Contract
FNVW	Waive Contract

FNWF   WF Loans Release: List of Work Items
FNWF_REP   Release Workflow: Synchronization
FNWO   Loans: Fast Processing
FNWS   Housing statistics
FNX1   Rollover: Create Table
FNX2   Rollover: Change Table
FNX3   Rollover: Display Table
FNX6   Rollover: Delete Table
FNX7   Rollover: Deactivate Table
FNX8   Rollover: Print Table
FNXD   TR-EDT: Documentation
FNXG   List of Bus. Partners Transferred
FNXU   List of Imported Loans
FNY1   New Business: Create Table
FNY2   New Business: Change Table
FNY3   New Business: Display Table
FNY6   New Business: Delete Table
FNY7   New Business: Deactivate Table
FNY8   New Business: Print Table
FNZ0   Rejections report
FNZ1   Postprocessing payment transactions
FNZA   Account Determination Customizing
FN_1   Table maint. transferred loans
FN_2   Table maintenance transf. partner

FN_UPD_FELDAUSW   Update Program for Field Selection

INDEX

SAP FI/CO Interview Questions

Attention SAP Experts

Writing a book can be the best thing for your career.

Have you ever considered writing a book in your area of SAP? Equity Press is the leading provider of knowledge products in SAP applications consulting, development, and support. If you have a manuscript or an idea of a manuscript, we'd love to help you get it published!

Please send your manuscript or manuscript ideas to **jim@sapcookbook.com** – we'll help you turn your dream into a reality.

Or mail your inquiries to:

Equity Press Manuscripts
BOX 706
Riverside, California
92502

Tel (951)788-0810
Fax (951)788-0812

50% Off your next SAPCOOKBOOK order

If you plan of placing an order for 10 or more books from www.sapcookbook.com you qualify for volume discounts. Please send an email to books@sapcookbook.com or phone 951-788-0810 to place your order.

You can also fax your orders to 951-788-0812

Interview books are great for cross-training

In the new global economy, the more you know the better. The sharpest consultants are doing everything they can to pick up more than one functional area of SAP. Each of the following Certification Review / Interview Question books provides an excellent starting point for your module learning and investigation. These books get you started like no other book can – by providing you the information that you really need to know, and fast.

SAPCOOKBOOK Interview Questions, Answers, and Explanations

ABAP - SAP ABAP Certification Review: SAP ABAP Interview Questions, Answers, and Explanations

SD - SAP SD Interview Questions, Answers, and Explanations

Security - SAP Security: SAP Security Essentials

HR - mySAP HR Interview Questions, Answers, and Explanations: SAP HR Certification Review

BW - SAP BW Ultimate Interview Questions, Answers, and Explanations: SAW BW Certification Review

SAP SRM Interview Questions Answers and Explanations

Basis - SAP Basis Certification Questions: Basis Interview Questions, Answers, and Explanations

MM - SAP MM Certification and Interview Questions: SAP MM Interview Questions, Answers, and Explanations

SAP BW Ultimate Interview Questions, Answers, and Explanations

Key Topics Include

• The most important BW settings to know
• BW tables and transaction code quick references
• Certification Examination Questions
• Extraction, Modeling and Configuration
• Transformations and Administration
• Performance Tuning, Tips & Tricks, and FAQ
• Everything a BW resource needs to know before an interview

mySAP HR Interview Questions, Answers, and Explanations

Key topics include:

• The most important HR settings to know
• mySAP HR Administration tables and transaction code quick references
• SAP HR Certification Examination Questions
• Org plan, Compensation, Year End, Wages, and Taxes
• User Management, Transport System, Patches, and Upgrades
• Benefits, Holidays, Payroll, and Infotypes
• Everything an HR resource needs to know before an interview

SAP SRM Interview Questions, Answers, and Explanations

Key Topics Include

-The most important SRM Configuration to know
-Common EBP Implementation Scenarios
-Purchasing Document Approval Processes
-Supplier Self Registration and Self Service (SUS)
-Live Auctions and Bidding Engine, RFX Processes (LAC)
-Details for Business Intelligence and Spend Analysis
-EBP Technical and Troubleshooting Information

SAP MM Interview Questions, Answers, and Explanations

- The most important MM Configuration to know
- Common MM Implementation Scenarios
- MM Certification Exam Questions
- Consumption Based Planning
- Warehouse Management
- Material Master Creation and Planning
- Purchasing Document Inforecords

SAP SD Interview Questions, Answers, and Explanations

• The most important SD settings to know
• SAP SD administration tables and transaction code quick references
• SAP SD Certification Examination Questions
• Sales Organization and Document Flow Introduction
• Partner Procedures, Backorder Processing, Sales BOM
• Backorder Processing, Third Party Ordering, Rebates and Refunds
• Everything an SD resource needs to know before an interview

SAP Basis Interview Questions, Answers, and Explanations

• The most important Basis settings to know
• Basis Administration tables and transaction code quick references
• Certification Examination Quest ions
• Oracle database, UNIX, and MS Windows Technical Information
• User Management, Transport System, Patches, and Upgrades
• Backup and Restore, Archiving, Disaster Recover, and Security
• Everything a Basis resource needs to know before an interview

SAP Security Essentials

- Finding Audit Critical Combinations
- Authentication, Transaction Logging, and Passwords
- Roles, Profiles, and User Management
- ITAR, DCAA, DCMA, and Audit Requirements
- The most important security settings to know
- Security Tuning, Tips & Tricks, and FAQ
- Transaction code list and table name references

SAP Workflow Interview Questions, Answers, and Explanations

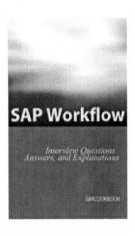

- Database Updates and Changing the Standard
- List Processing, Internal Tables, and ALV Grid Control
- Dialog Programming, ABAP Objects
- Data Transfer, Basis Administration
- ABAP Development reference updated for 2006!
- Everything an ABAP resource needs to know before an interview

Printed in the United Kingdom
by Lightning Source UK Ltd.
125659UK00001B/188/A